# ON THE HORIZON

# LOIS LOWRY

Illustrated by
KENARD PAK

CLARION BOOKS
AN IMPRINT OF HARPERCOLLINSPUBLISHERS

Clarion Books is an imprint of HarperCollins Publishers.

On the Horizon
Text copyright © 2020 by Lois Lowry
Illustrations copyright © 2020 by Kenard Pak

Library of Congress Cataloging-in-Publication Data
Names: Lowry, Lois, author. | Pak, Kenard, illustrator.
Title: On the horizon / Lois Lowry ; illustrated by Kenard Pak.
Description: Boston : Houghton Mifflin Harcourt, [2020] | Audience: Ages:
10–12 | Audience: Grades: 4–6 | Summary: "From two-time Newbery medalist
and living legend Lois Lowry comes a moving account of the lives lost in
two of WWII's most infamous events: Pearl Harbor and Hiroshima. With
evocative black-and-white illustrations by SCBWI Golden Kite Award
winner Kenard Pak." —Provided by publisher.
Identifiers: LCCN 2019008795 (print) | LCCN 2019980713 (ebook)
Subjects: LCSH: Lowry, Lois—Childhood and youth—Juvenile literature. |
World War, 1939–1945—Casualties—Juvenile literature. | Pearl Harbor
(Hawaii), Attack on, 1941—Juvenile literature. | World War,
1939–1945—Hawaii—Juvenile literature. | World War,
1939–1945—Japan—Hiroshima-shi—Juvenile literature. | World War,
1939–1945—Personal narratives, American—Juvenile literature. |
Hiroshima-shi (Japan)—History—Bombardment, 1945—Juvenile literature.
Classification: LCC D743.7 .L69 2020 (print) | LCC D743.7 (ebook) |
DDC 940.54/25219540922—dc23
LC record available at https://lccn.loc.gov/2019008795
LC ebook record available at https://lccn.loc.gov/2019980713

ISBN 978-0-35-812940-0 hardcover
ISBN 978-0-35-866807-7 paperback

The illustrations in this book were done in pencil and edited digitally.
Typography by Whitney Leader-Picone

22  23  24  25  26   PC/LSCC   10  9  8  7  6  5  4  3  2  1

First paperback edition, 2022

*For Howard, with love*

# Part 1.

# ON THE HORIZON

On December 7, 1941, early on a Sunday morning, Japanese planes bombed Pearl Harbor, in Hawaii. Most of the United States Pacific Fleet was moored there. Tremendous damage was inflicted, and the battleship *Arizona* sank within minutes, with a loss of 1,177 men.

The bombing of Pearl Harbor that day was the beginning, for the United States, of World War II.

I was born in Honolulu in 1937. Years later, as I watched a home movie taken by my father in 1940, I realized that as I played on the beach at Waikiki, USS *Arizona* could be seen through mist in the background, on the horizon.

# THAT MORNING

They had named the battleships for states:

*Arizona*
*Pennsylvania*
*West Virginia*
*Nevada*
*Oklahoma*
*Tennessee*
*California*
*Maryland*

They called them "she"
as if they were women
(gray metal women),
and they were all there that morning
in what they called Battleship Row.

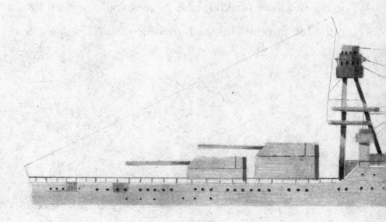

Their places
(the places of the gray metal women)
were called berths.

*Arizona* was at berth F-7.
On either side, her nurturing sisters:
*Nevada*
and *Tennessee*.

The sisters, wounded, survived.
But *Arizona*, her massive body sheared,
slipped down. She disappeared.

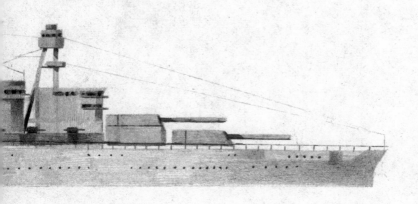

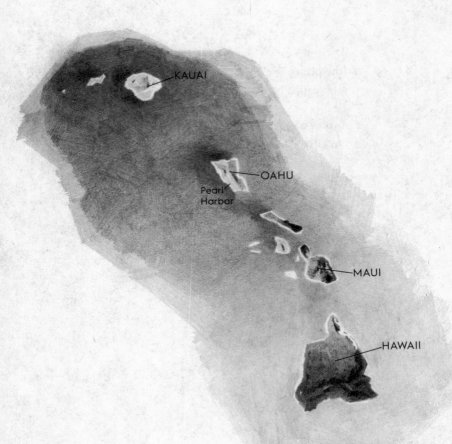

# RAINBOWS

It was an island of rainbows.
My mother said that color arced across the sky
on the spring day when I was born.

On the island of rainbows,
my bare feet slipping in sand,
I learned to walk.

And to talk:
My Hawaiian nursemaid
taught me her words, with their soft vowels:
*humuhumunukunukuāpua`a,*
the name of a little fish!
It made me laugh, to say it.
We laughed together.

*Ānuenue* meant "rainbow."
Were there rainbows that morning?
I suppose there must have been:
bright colors, as the planes came in.

# ALOHA

My grandmother visited.
She had come by train across the broad land
from her home in Wisconsin, and then by ship.
We met her and heaped wreaths
of plumeria around her neck.
"*Aloha*," we said to her.
*Welcome. Hello.*

I called her Nonny.
She took me down by the ocean.
The sea moved in a blue-green rhythm, soft against the sand.
We played there, she and I, with a small shovel,
and laughed when the breeze caught my bonnet
and lifted it from my blond hair.

We played and giggled: calm, serene.
And there behind us—slow, unseen—
*Arizona*, great gray tomb,
moved, majestic, toward her doom.

# SHE WAS THERE

We never saw the ship.
But she was there.

She was moving slowly
on the horizon, shrouded in the mist
that separated skies from seas
while we laughed, unknowing, in the breeze.

She carried more than
twelve hundred men
on deck, or working down below.
We didn't look up. We didn't know.

# LEO AMUNDSON

Leo was just seventeen.
He'd enlisted in July.
The U.S. Marines! He must have been proud.
And his folks, too: Scandinavian stock.
Immigrants to Wisconsin, like my own grandparents.
Leo was from La Crosse. My father was born there.
My Nonny had come from La Crosse by train.
Had she known Leo's parents?
Had she nodded to Mrs. Amundson on the street?
Had she said, "Good morning. I hear your boy's a Marine now"?

Nonny and I played on the beach in the sunshine.
On the horizon, the boy from La Crosse
(just seventeen),
service number 309872,
was on the ship. We never knew.

# GEORGE AND JIMMIE

George and Jimmie Bromley,
brothers from Tacoma,
handsome boys with curly hair.
(Jimmie was the older, but not by much.)

There were thirty-seven sets of brothers aboard
(one set was twins).
And a father and son,
Texans: Thomas Free and his
seventeen-year-old boy, William.
Both gone. Both lost.

They found George Bromley's body.
Not Jimmie's, though.

# *SOLACE*

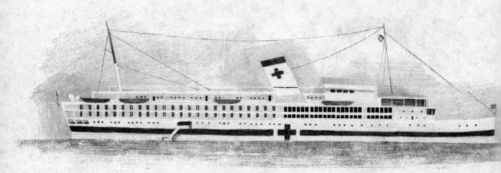

The hospital ships had names that spoke of need:

*Comfort*
*Hope*
*Solace*
*Mercy*
*Refuge*

They carried the wounded and ill.

That morning, *Solace* was moored near the *Arizona*.

She sent her launches and stretchers across.
The harbor had a film of burning oil.
Scorched men were pulled one by one from the flames
and taken to *Solace*.

# JAKE AND JOHN ANDERSON

John Anderson survived the attack.
He'd been preparing for church.
Rescued, he asked to go back.
He begged to return, to search.

He was burned and bleeding.
"My brother's still there," he said,
distraught, desperate, and pleading.
"Jake's there! I know he's not dead!"

But one would die, and one live on.
Identical twins. Jake and John.

# BIRTHDAY

Everett Reid turned twenty-four
December sixth, the day before.

He held the rank machinist's mate.
He'd celebrated, stayed out late

with friends; they'd danced and sung.
He lived ashore. He'd married young.

In the morning, when he woke,
he heard the sirens, saw the smoke.

He'd remember all his life
the hasty parting from his wife,

her quick and terrified embrace,
his frantic journey to the base.

His birthdays, though, for many years
brought no joy. Just grief. Just tears.

# THE BEACH

The morning beach was deserted.
We were alone, Nonny and me
(and Daddy, his camera whirring).

I tiptoed, pranced, and flirted
with waves. Just we three
and empty beach. Nothing stirring.

And if we'd looked? And been alerted
to a gray ship at the edge of the sea?
The mist would still have been there, blurring

the shape of a ship moving slowly.
Now, years later, it seems holy.

# THE BAND

NBU 22. That's what it was called:
Navy Band Unit 22. The *Arizona* band.
That morning—it was not yet eight—
they were on deck, about to play.
(Their music raised the flag each day.)

When the alert came,
they ran to their battle station—
they called it the black powder room.
Their job was to pass ammunition
to the gunners. But the black powder exploded.

Twenty-one young men, prepared
for morning colors. Not one was spared.

All the high-stepping boys
who'd marched at high school
football games, once; who'd enlisted;
now, with their instruments, lay twisted.

# THE MUSICIANS

Neal Radford: At twenty-six,
Neal was the oldest among
the musicians. The others
were all so very young,

like Alexander Nadel—don't forget
he went to Juilliard! But was still
just twenty. He played cornet.
So did the youngest, that was Bill
McCary, southern boy, seventeen.
An only child from Birmingham,
Billy was eager, bright, and keen
to give his all for Uncle Sam.

Music was their main pursuit.
Curtis Haas—they called him Curt—
played clarinet, tenor sax, and flute.
A handsome kid: a clown, a flirt.
Each band member was, like him,
such a source of family pride.
Curt was young, hardworking, trim;
twenty-one the day he died.

Back home each one had friends they missed,
dogs they'd raised, and girls they'd kissed;
childhood rooms with model planes,
boyhood bikes with rusted chains;
moms and dads and baseball teams,
and dreams—each one of them had dreams.

# CAPTAIN KIDD

It sounds like the name of a pirate.
Nonny told me stories of pirates,
of trolls, and dragons, and kings.
Imaginary things.

He was not an imaginary hero.
He was Captain Isaac Campbell Kidd,
commanding officer of USS *Arizona*.
His friends called him Cap.

When he was made commander
of the entire Battleship Division,
he became an admiral.

Admiral Kidd ran to the bridge
that morning in December.

His Naval Academy ring
was found melted and fused to the mast.
It is not an imaginary thing,
a symbol of devotion so vast.

# JAMES MYERS

James was from Missouri
and had two brothers.
The older boy had died in France
in World War I.
The youngest (out in a field,
bringing in the cows, when a storm struck)
was killed by lightning.
He was fifteen.

So James was left.
He married, and had two sons himself.
But his wife died young, and
the little boys, Jimmy and Gordon,
went to live with their grandma in Seattle.
It was the other grandma,
widowed Mary Myers, in Missouri,
who opened the telegram with dread.
"I had bad luck with all my boys," she said.

# SILAS WAINWRIGHT

Popular kid, Silas. Played football
in high school. Joined everything.
He wanted to be a doctor.

But times were tough.
And Silas was the oldest
of eleven children.
No college for him.
He worked on the family farm.
Then, at twenty, he enlisted.

The navy made him a
pharmacist's mate.
He learned to do minor surgery.
It was as close as he could get
to medicine.

Back home, in his
small New York town,
friends got Christmas cards
that year from Silas.

He'd mailed them nine days
before he died.

# 8:15, DECEMBER 1941

Frank Cabiness, PFC,
survived. From his station
in the mainmast high above,
he looked down
and saw that half of his ship
was gone.

His hands were burned.
Not like his shipmates',
charred by flaming oil;
his were friction burns. Grasping
ropes and ladders, he slid down eighty feet
to save himself that morning.

His watch (his children have it still)
stopped at 8:15.
Time doesn't matter now, to Frank.
At eighty-six, he returned to his ship.
Divers took his ashes down
and placed them in the fourth gun turret,
where he would rest with his shipmates.

A bugler played taps
as they took the urn and dove.

# THE FOURTH TURRET

One by one, the divers
have carried their ashes below
and placed them in the fourth turret.

John Anderson—remember him?
The one who lost his identical twin?

John reached the age of ninety-eight.
Many, many years had passed.
Remembering his brother's fate,
he asked to be with Jake at last.

# CHILD ON A BEACH

I was a child who played in the sand,
a little shovel in my hand;
I pranced and giggled. I was three.
The ship sailed past. I didn't see.

I wonder, now that time's gone by,
about that day: the sea, the sky . . .
the day I frolicked in the foam,
when Honolulu was my home.

I think back to that sunlit day
when I was young, and so were they.
If I had noticed? If I'd known?
Would each of us be less alone?

I've traveled many miles since then—
around the world, and back again;
I've learned that there will always be
things we miss, that we don't see

on the horizon. Things beyond.
And yet there is a lasting bond
between us, linking each to each:
Boys on a ship. Child on a beach.

# PEARL HARBOR

*triolet*

Time will not age them. They are boys still:
young in that December, and young today.
Though others of us falter, shrink, fall ill,
time will not age them. They are boys still.
We'll pause, remember, grieve for them, until
memories fade. But though our hair turns gray,
time will not age them. They are boys still:
young in that December, and young today.

# Part 2.

# ANOTHER HORIZON

At 8:15 in the morning, on August 6, 1945, an American plane dropped an atomic bomb on the city of Hiroshima in southern Japan. The city was destroyed. Some eighty thousand people died that day, and thousands more, afflicted with radiation sickness, died in the following weeks, months, and years.

Ultimately, the atomic bomb brought about the end of World War II.

# NAMES

Code-named "Little Boy," the bomb
was placed aboard. The men were calm.

They flew six hours. The skies were clear.
They'd arm the bomb when they drew near.

The plane was named *Enola Gay*.
It carried a whole crew that day:

George. Tom. Wyatt. Joe.
Dutch. Jake. *Six hours to go*.

Two Roberts. Morris. Richard. Deak.
They waited, watching; didn't speak

until the order came: *Deploy*.
*Time to release Little Boy.*

At 8:15 they let it fall.
The bomber pilot's name was Paul.

He'd named the airplane for his mom.
It carried twelve men and the bomb.

*Six hours back.* No talk, still. None.
Except: *My God. What have we done?*

# JAPANESE MORNING

In a small town called Tabuse
on August sixth, a summer day,
a little boy, Koichi Seii,
felt a shudder in the earth
and saw the sky
change.

From Hiroshima, miles away,
beyond the hills, beside the bay,
on August sixth, a summer day,
Koichi-san perceived the birth
of something
strange.

Is this how it ends? The world? This way?
On August sixth? A summer day?
Morning light? A boy at play?
It could. It might. It may.

# THE CLOUD

They likened it, later,
because of its shape,
to a mushroom.

Think of mushrooms:
fragile,
ascending and unfurling
after a rain,
rising on ragged stems
through damp moss.

Think of this cloud:
savage,
ripping sky and earth
and future,
spawning death
with its spore.

# AFTERWARD

*haiku*

White light, whirling cloud
Next a strange ghostly silence
Then startling black rain

# TAKEO

School was about to begin
for Takeo and his friends.
As they waited, they played
hide-and-seek. Takeo was It.

He covered his eyes and counted,
*Ichi, ni,*
*san, shi . . .*
A blinding light came. A roar. A vibration.
And after that, silence.

A soldier, searching for survivors,
heard his cries, dug through rubble,
found him, picked him up, carried him
through the silent, ruined city.

He heard his name. *Takeo-san! Takeo-san!*
"It's my daddy!" he said to the soldier.
There, on the bridge, in the silence,
he was placed in his father's arms.

Later, he remembered his father's tears,
and how he had bowed to the soldier,
whispering, "Thank you," over and over.

# THE RED TRICYCLE

Soon four years old! A big boy!
Shinichi Tetsutani
played that morning,
riding his red tricycle.

When his parents found him,
he was still gripping the
handlebar. He was so proud
of his red tricycle.

Shin-chan, they called him.
They buried him in the garden,
and with him, they buried
his red tricycle.

He had called it his friend.
*Tomodachi.*

# TRAM GIRLS

The country had been at war for a long time.
Most of the men had gone to serve.
Teenagers were called upon to fill their jobs.
High school girls learned to operate
the trams that moved through the city.
They felt useful and proud.

Schoolboys thought that Tram 101
had the best-looking girls.
They always waited for that one.

None of that mattered
when it happened—the bright light,
the explosion,
the engines fell silent.

Akira Ishida thought it was her fault,
that she had done something wrong,
caused an accident.
Then she looked to the street,
where crowds had been walking.
There was no one there. No one left.
They were vaporized.

She was a young girl with
a singed uniform, and
a lifetime
of nightmares.

# SADAKO SASAKI

Legend says that if you fold one thousand
paper cranes, a wish will be granted.
Sadako believed that.
She folded and folded.

She was two
on that August morning,
at home when the bomb fell,
and she seemed uninjured.

But the black rain fell on her,
carrying radiation.

She folded and folded,
there in the hospital.
She was twelve when she died,
surrounded by small paper birds.

# CHIEKO SUETOMO

Chieko survived.
Later, she found her doll,
the Shirley Temple doll that her father
had brought her from a trip to the USA.

The doll's curls were singed,
her pink dress charred.
But her dimpled face
still smiled, unscarred.

# THE TRICYCLE

They had buried it with him,
the red tricycle
that he called his friend.

And forty years passed.
He was three.
Now he would be a man.

When his parents felt ready,
his father, old now, dug in the garden.
Gently they took his small bones

and moved them to a family grave.
His friend, the tricycle?
It rests now in a museum.

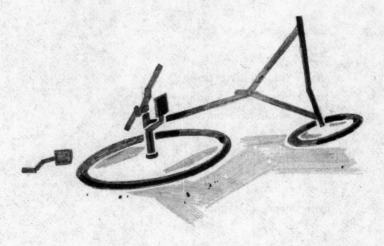

# 8:15, AUGUST 1945

Shinji Mikamo was helping his father
that morning.
He remembered that it was a hot day.
He was up on the roof.
He had raised his arm to wipe the sweat
from his forehead, when he saw
the blinding flash.

His father had just called to him
to stop daydreaming.
Was this part of a dream?
Then came a thundering roar,
and he was thrown under the collapsing house.

Two months later, at last
able to walk again, Shinji left
the hospital and made his way home,
looking for his father.
He never saw him again.
But he found, in the ruins,
his father's watch. 8:15, it said.

# HIROSHIMA

*triolet*

The cloud appeared over the distant hill,
blossoming like strange new flowers in spring,
opening, growing. But the world was still.
When the cloud appeared over the distant hill,
silence had fallen. There were no sounds until
rain came. Not true rain, but black drops falling
from the cloud that appeared over a distant hill,
blossoming like strange new flowers in spring.

# Part 3.

# BEYOND THE HORIZONS

After we left Hawaii, I lived with my mother and my sister and brother in a small Pennsylvania town throughout World War II. My father was gone for most of the war. For many of those months, he served on the hospital ship *Hope*. Then he found himself on an island called Tinian. He didn't know this—it was very secret—but on that island, they loaded the atomic bomb into the plane that would fly to Hiroshima.

After the war ended, my dad remained in Japan, on the staff of the hospital in Tokyo. Finally, when I was eleven, we joined him there. We went by ship from New York—down through the Panama Canal, then up the coast of California, stopping for other passengers in San Francisco, and finally across the Pacific Ocean.

It was a very long trip. When we arrived, my father met us and drove us to our new home in Tokyo. On the way, he whispered to me that he had a surprise waiting for me there.

It was a green bicycle.

# MEIJI

So much had been destroyed.
Some places were rubble.
But near my home, in Shibuya,
I would ride my bicycle to the
Great Torii of Meiji Shrine.

Inside the temple grounds,
ancient trees still stood.
People walked slowly
and were quiet.

Beyond the walls,
the sounds of the city continued.
The rubble remained.
But within that gate,
everything was hushed
and unbroken.

# AFTER THAT MORNING

After the August morning
when the bright light
seared Hiroshima
into nothingness,

Koichi Seii, now eight,
had left his home
where the sky and air
still shimmered with death,

and gone north with his
mother and sister.
They would find their way
to the city of Tokyo,

to the area called Shibuya,
and begin a new life there.
They would start again.
The war had ended.

# BON ODORI

In summer, during Obon Festival,
the drumming began, and chanting.
I watched everyone—
grandparents, children—
moving, circling,
in the Bon Odori dance.

From the shadows
where I watched,
my bike against a tree,
I moved my arms as they did:
up, and forward, and then:
Clap. Clap. Pause. And: Clap.
Gracefully they moved,
honoring their ancestors.

So did I.

# HIBAKUSHA

In summer I went to the Inland Sea
and saw a hill with a stunted tree.
The *jima*—islands—rose with grace,
but wind misshaped things in this place.

Not far from the island where I stood,
where the tree displayed its twisted wood,
a ruined city curved the shore,
its name synonymous with war:

*Hiroshima*

Like wind-warped pine, its people, too,
were twisted, broken, scarred, askew.
But like the trees, they lived. They thrived.
Their name means "those who have survived":

*Hibakusha*

# INVISIBLE

Back in Pennsylvania, where I had lived,
there was a comic book
called *Invisible Scarlet O'Neil*.

I loved Scarlet. She could magically
make herself invisible.
And now: I could too.

I rode my green bike
through the busy streets of Shibuya,
where children ran and laughed,

babies cried, dogs barked,
shopkeepers chattered and called, and
oxen lumbered through the streets

pulling carts of fertilizer.
And I watched and listened,
feeling invisible

on my green bike,
until the day that a woman
touched my hair and spoke.

# THE WORD FOR "HATE"

I rode the green bike home that day,
humiliated. I told the maids—
Ritsuko, Teruko, Aiko—
that a woman had touched my hair
and said she hated me.

They were shocked.
*What word?*
I repeated the word that meant "hate."
"*Kirai*," I told them.

They whispered among themselves.
Then they asked:
*Maybe "kirei"?*

*Well, maybe.*
*Isn't it the same word?*

They laughed. *No. Not at all.*
*She said you were pretty.*

Such a simple shift of sound!
My mistake was so profound:
When the woman touched my hair
(though I'd pretended not to care),
I'd felt suffused by shame
and guilt. Reproach. And blame.

# GIRL ON A BIKE

Beside a school I paused one day
and watched some children run and play.
We were curious. I know that's true.
Their eyes were dark and mine were blue.

I braked my bike and watched them there.
I saw them eye my pale blond hair.
They looked at me, and I at them. So why
were we so silent: mute and shy?

I smiled before I rode away
but never met Koichi Seii

until so many years went by
that he was gray-haired, so was I.

I'd lived in his country, then.
And now he'd moved to mine, so when
we met (his name was Allen now),
we mused and pondered how

from our horizons we had viewed
a war begin, a war conclude.
We were young. We were alike.
Boy in a schoolyard. Girl on a bike.

# GAIJIN

Aoyama Gakuin, not far away,
was where I stopped my bike that day,
as on its grounds Koichi played
and watched me. Was he afraid?

*Gakuin* meant school. I knew words now,
in Japanese, especially how
*tomodachi* was the word for "friend." Why
did it seem wrong for us to try

for friendship? Was it just too soon?
I pedaled home that afternoon
feeling *gaijin:* foreign, weird;
feeling different, feeling feared.

# NOW

I stand beside Japanese tourists
looking down at the *Arizona*.
They look stricken. They bow.
Their bows are deep.

From the dark split hull below,
oil still bubbles to the surface
as if she breathes.
As if asleep.

In Hiroshima,
at the memorial there,
in front of the blackened tricycle,
I too bow. I weep.

友達

# TOMODACHI

*triolet*

We could not be friends. Not then. Not yet.
Until the cloud dispersed and cleared,
we needed time to mend, forget.
We could not be friends. Not then. Not yet.
Till years had passed, until we met
and understood the things we'd feared,
we could not be friends. Not then. Not yet.
Until the cloud dispersed and cleared.

# AUTHOR'S NOTE

When I was a child, in the days when there was no television, it was always a treat when we could talk Daddy into setting up the projector and screen and showing the home movies one more time. Mother would darken the room, and we watched the so-familiar scenes: me learning to walk; our grandmother arriving to visit us in Hawaii and smiling as leis of flowers were heaped around her neck; my sister, Helen, in her Halloween clown costume; me again, on the beach now with a little shovel; and finally, the two of us, barefoot, watering Mother's flowers in the garden.

When I was eleven, we moved to Tokyo and the home movies went into storage along with our furniture. Time passed, and now I was a teenager in New York. It was the fifties. My family got a television, and I don't think we ever looked at Dad's movies again. Until . . .

It was 1980. Dad was getting old now and living with my mother in Virginia. I lived in Boston, and one time when I visited my parents, Dad showed me the circular metal containers that held those old bits of my early childhood and mused that he probably should throw the deteriorating films away.

But instead I took them back to Boston with me and found someone who could save them to a videotape. I had recently bought a VCR—something that was quite new at the time—and one night, with company there, I slipped the tape into the VCR and we watched the scenes from my childhood. There was Helen in her clown suit again. I played once more on the beach at Waiki-ki, and the breeze lifted my sun hat as I grabbed at it, laughing. Then, barefoot, we began to water our mother's flowers one more time.

"Wait," my friend John said suddenly. "Pause it and go back to the beach scene."

I did so. John was a Boston lawyer, but he was an Annapolis graduate and had had a previous career as the captain of a nuclear submarine. He leaned forward as we watched the beach scene again. Then he said, "Look on the horizon. That's the *Arizona.*"

The room of people fell silent because now we were no longer watching a small story of a little girl playing with a shovel in 1940. We were watching a huge piece of history. The *Arizona* carried 1,200 men. Almost all of them would soon be dead.

I am still haunted by that. By the fact that I had giggled and scampered in the sand on that day, while in the background—on the horizon—the doomed young men had moved slowly across the landscape that was my life as well as theirs.

\* \* \*

In 1994 I met the brilliant and gifted illustrator Allen Say. We had breakfast together during a library convention in Miami and discovered that not only were we born the same year (*You're much older*, Allen said smugly. *By five months*, I scoffed), but that we had lived near each other in Tokyo when we were children, in the days when he was still Koichi Seii, whose family had fled southern Japan in 1945. Amazingly, he remembered that a girl on a green bike had once paused and watched him and his classmates on their school playground in Shibuya.

"Me," I confessed.

"You," he acknowledged, laughing.


That same year, I took my eleven-year-old grandson, Jamie, to Hawaii for a vacation, just the two of us. I showed him the hospital where I'd been born and the place where my family had lived just outside of Honolulu. Then we went to Pearl Harbor.

It was on the USS *Arizona* Memorial, as we stood in the midst of a hushed crowd, that something caught our attention. In front of the engraved list of names—those who had died, those who still lay below us on the sunken vessel—was a small glass jar containing a few flowers. A note propped beside it said *For my grandpa* and followed that message with a name. Jamie and I read the name, then found it in the list of doomed men. We did the math, whispering to each other. That young sailor had left a child, we realized. The child had grown up and had a child of his own. *That* child had left these flowers for the grandfather he had never had a chance to meet.

My grandson and I moved to the side and stood there looking at the sea, almost overwhelmed by the way history had become real, and watching the slow formation of oily bubbles that still, after so many years, oozed their way to the surface.

It has taken many years for me to put these things together, to try to find some meaning in the way lives intersect—or how they fail to. I guess the important thing is also the simplest: to acknowledge our connectedness on this earth; to bow our heads when we see a scorched tricycle or a child's message to his lost grandpa; and to honor the past by making silent promises to our fellow humans that we will work for a better and more peaceful future.